AVEN MOD

Run Covid Run Away

Ride with me as I chase Covid away! Let's Go!

D1518163

Copyright © 2022 by Aven Mod

All rights reserved. No part of this publication may be reproduced, stored or transmitted in any form or by any means, electronic, mechanical, photocopying, recording, scanning, or otherwise without written permission from the publisher. It is illegal to copy this book, post it to a website, or distribute it by any other means without permission.

Aven Mod asserts the moral right to be identified as the author of this work.

Aven Mod has no responsibility for the persistence or accuracy of URLs for external or third-party Internet Websites referred to in this publication and does not guarantee that any content on such Websites is, or will remain, accurate or appropriate.

Designations used by companies to distinguish their products are often claimed as trademarks. All brand names and product names used in this book and on its cover are trade names, service marks, trademarks and registered trademarks of their respective owners. The publishers and the book are not associated with any product or vendor mentioned in this book. None of the companies referenced within the book have endorsed the book.

First edition

This book was professionally typeset on Reedsy.
Find out more at reedsy.com

For Grace, Nina & Joe
and for
Laura

The Love that we lost

Contents

Acknowledgement

The wonderful Elgin, IL Emergency Services, Paramedic, Police and Fire Departments.

The fantastic staff at Northwestern Medical Delnor Hospital.

All of my primary care physicians and staff.

My immediate and extended family, friends and neighbors who were always there.

The Mikkelsen Twins for showing me it can be done!

To you the reader for making this possible.

1

Introduction

Hello and welcome to my Covid journey! Please join me as I recount my first-hand experience on contracting Covid, leading to Covid Pneumonia and fighting off a NDE (Near Death Experience, I know, like the world needs another acronym!) I'm glad you're here with me, and I hope sharing my experiences will enlighten you on the treatments and information that came out of my situation.

Using my own satirical, humorous way of storytelling and thinking, I want to make you smile while riding along with me and lessen the fear of the unknown for you. My goal is for you to gain some knowledge and understanding to educate yourself and develop an appreciation for all those who work in the emergency services & response, and medical fields as well.

My kids and family have had their brushes with contracting Covid over the past two plus years. Quarantining, wearing masks, cleaning groceries, disinfecting just about everything, and stress and panic attacks, have grasped us all, paralyzing our everyday way of life and activities. We've become afraid of touching anything, going outside, and even greeting people! I'm sure you've gone through this in some way, shape or form in your life. It creates an uneasy feeling in your body and mental state as you begin to question everything around. Social media also lends its hand at creating undue stress.

I can assure you that you are not alone. You can overcome the fear and anxiety you may have and do anything you set your mind to. "Easily said," you're saying to yourself and to me right now. NO! If my family and I can go through all the bullshit that life has thrown us and still come out fighting, you can too! Don't fool yourself into waiting for someone or something to come and change your life. It's YOU that is that person that can change your life.

What this is not…. It's not a political, either side of the aisle, rant. I am not here to sway your opinion, sway your vote, lay blame, argue either way on vaccination or claim that I have undiscovered the truth about Covid or any other mass media or conspiracy theory! If aliens are indeed real, I hope that they can't contract Covid at least. Oh yeah, there's a hospital stay too. Let's mask up (sorry) and dig in!

2

A Covid bout goes how many rounds?

I have 2 daughters and a son, in that order, currently ranging in age from 23 to 19 and each have their own opinions on Covid (and life and _my_ money) but the one thing they all have in common is that they've battled it, twice each for my daughters. When tragedy struck with the sudden illness of their mother years ago, they were forced to take on mature responsibilities at a very young age that most children never have to. I admire them for that and understand all the emotional and anguish that they still carry with them and must deal with. Plus, during Covid quarantine, having a sick parent that you can't see in person, touch and hold had to be difficult for my daughters as during this time as they shared an apartment away from home while going to school and working.

I will need to preface something here. A tie into what I consider a "comorbidity." My wife had been ill for over 5 years since 2017 and I, my kids and family (including a superhuman aunt) took care of her. This is another story for another time, another place. The extenuating circumstances, or comorbidities, that I'm referring to are mental, emotional, and physical drains. I was burning the candle at both ends and then started to melt the candle to the wick in the center creating two separate candles burning at each end and so on and so on!

Two plus years of hiding and looking over our shoulders. Will the fight ever end? Is it going to be a knockout? My son is where my story comes to fruition as we build off his Covid case.

3

Sadness Stress and Sickness

My wife, oldest sister and aunt all passed on in November or 2021. A very rough month for sure and as I said before, that's another story for another time. These events became an amplification for my battle with anxiety, stress and eventually breaking down my immune system and contracting Covid. They chipped away at me as I tried to get any form of rest or relief. Body, mind, and spirit all taxed at once.

As a family, with the wakes and funerals all within a short time, we were obviously exposed to several people, both the same family members repeatedly and many, many others as well. Most restrictions were lifted at this point and though these were not super spreader events, we all were hesitant to kiss anyone on any cheek, buttock, or lip. Handshakes turned into fist pumps and elbow jabs; hand sanitizer was everywhere and, if someone coughed or sneezed, you'd expect a Racing Team Pit Crew to show up and disinfect a 6-foot circle around them and hose them off with a commercial grade insecticide.

The Thanksgiving holiday without our loved ones was a tough holiday for my family and especially for my kids and me. This would be only a week from my wife's passing and the first Holiday without her in nearly

30 years. It was difficult for sure. We truly appreciate our family doing their best for us. Have you ever had that feeling of looking for someone that you know is always there and realize that they'll never be there again? Take that feeling, multiply it by a million then add in a hefty gut punch plus a wave of body aches and you're close to knowing how that feels.

Shortly after the holiday weekend, my son began to feel ill. He started with a persistent cough, nasal activity and feeling achy and sore all over. Obviously, this raised concern for us, so we contacted our primary care physician who ordered a full Covid test for him.

We didn't have any access to home tests at this point and there were none available in the stores. During that second week of December 2021, I took my son to one of those stand-up remote, sit in your car, Covid Rapid and PCR testing facilities. They're kind of like those gas-station or vacant corners where vans park and sell t-shirts, blankets or velvet Elvis paintings. My oldest daughter was now staying with us, and she went to another test facility as she was quarantining far away from my son and me. The immediate nasal rapid test came back positive for him – but not for me. "Dodged a bullet there" I thought, as I must keep working and stay strong for my family. Keep in mind though I had a mask on, I was sitting next to him in the car for a long period of time.

Shortly after that we took him to the hospital for another "official" rapid and PCR test that was ordered for him. Rapid results were positive. Over the next few days, we learned that his hospital PCR came back positive, and then the quarantine we were in, went into full force. By the way, we finally received both of our PCR results from the outdoor facility in March of 2022, over two months after we took them. He was positive of course and mine came back negative. Big, Frigging, Deal.

During that week of December, I informed my workplace that I have been exposed to Covid and my son tested positive. Fortunately, I was able to work out of my home while taking care of my son. Thank goodness for my place of work and the owner allowing me to work from home. My daughter tested negative and vanished from the house, retreating to her boyfriend's apartment, and staying away as far as possible. Me? I felt fine and had no symptoms other than dry hands from using disinfectant wipes on everything so much! The basement became my son's dungeon as I worked the rest of the house.

Fast forward past my son's quarantine for about 2 weeks and we are now near the Christmas holiday. Daughter number one is back at home and we're all doing well. I developed a slight cough that I felt was more of a cold than anything else. I had no discomfort, no fatigue, no fever, etc. Work had instructed me to stay at home so as to not risk carrying the virus into the office and potentially ruining the holiday season for them all.

4

Happy New Year 2022

This is the year that, finally, all comes to an end with the virus, and we can start anew! What starts with a bang can end up exploding in your face. It's like getting too close to the toilet bowl when you're cleaning it and you flush the suds down but it backsplashes at you! Yuck!

We spent Christmas alone, missing my second daughter and all our family and parties. With the center of all our lives gone for just over a month, the holidays truly SUCKED! Around that time, I started not sleeping well. That last week of the year I found myself not being able to sleep much at all. I thought it was just my normal anxiety related to the stress of all the past years (especially from the last few months) culminating with deaths and all the million details that surrounds it. Keep in mind that my middle name has been "anxiety" for most of my life. I can ride the runaway train of anxiety at full speed. It's that old friend that sits right beside me. One thought runs away with another and another and on and on and on.

Though I did not feel severely ill at all, the lack of sleep issue grew worse. I contacted my physician's office and they set up a Covid test for me. I did have a virtual exam call with an online physician that led to a diagnosis of insomnia and, of course, the need to get tested for Covid which was my intention. As we were in the final days of December, I began to feel a bit worse with a headache, some aches, and pains but I could not put my finger on what was wrong. No fever, no running nose…just lack of sleep. My daughter and son tried to help me get some rest and get to sleep as best they could. It just wasn't happening as whenever I laid down, I could not relax at all.

5

Breathe In Breathe Out

Say "Hi" to New Year's Day! I sat on the couch and couldn't understand what was going on with me. My own personal anxiety was starting to take over and rule my day. All the medicines, coping mechanisms, and positive thoughts I had were going right down the drain. It almost felt like I was floating away (and I'm a big guy too). At this point, I thought to myself, since my wife was on Hospice until the end of her life, I have a wealth of tests, supplies and medical apparatuses in the house. Maybe my blood pressure was out of whack, or I was in arrhythmia, maybe I was experiencing mini strokes, what's my sugar level at, or some wild and exotic animal or bug had bitten me (Um, no....). So, lastly, without even thinking about it, I took my pulse ox using the pulse oximeter we had at home. This is a small device that you place on one of your fingers and it has a red-light beam that measures your oxygen saturation.

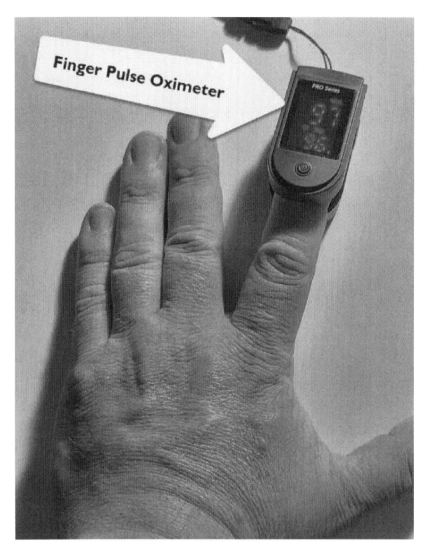

Finger Pulse Oximeter

Kaboom (or rather Kibosh)! Well, that did it – for sure. Apparently, a normal reading for a human being should be at least 95% saturation or better. The medical community would prefer you to be closer to 99%. I guess that a 72% reading is a failing grade. Yes, I told myself – it is.

I repeatedly took the reading repeatedly figuring that something was wrong with the oximeter. Then I had my daughter keep taking it. Note:

you should never compare a 20 something year old's health to someone 30 years older than them. I was now having her take her own reading. 99%, 98%, 99% and on. Crap. I read that the home units can be off by as much as a percent or two, but not 28%.

Now that I am in my early 50's (no I am not a "Boomer" as my children chide me about) and an overweight big guy, I have *NEVER* been admitted to or stayed overnight in a hospital over my entire life (except when I was born). Ok, an admission of guilt here and a sincere apology to my late wife (she did forgive me). I never stayed overnight in the hospital when my children were born. We were and are incredibly grateful and thankful that our children were not born with any serious issues. Each was a cesarean and when they and mom were settled in and getting rest – I went home to get some rest. HEY! It's not like I abandoned them, I only went home, slept, cleaned up and was right back to the hospital ASAP. Can we circle back here?

6

A New Year's Day Chicagoland Snowstorm

My second sister has always said that if "I didn't have bad luck, I'd have none at all." Naturally while all this is happening to me, the season's first major snowstorm hits on New Year's Day. It really screwed up everything - like when your cup of coffee is mixed just right and is at the perfect temperature to drink and your server comes over and tops off your cup. Don't get me wrong, I genuinely appreciate all the work they do, and I am a good tipper too, but now I have to start my mix all over again.

I sat on my couch thinking to myself, I feel like I'm breathing alright, but I can't draw in a full breath – or exhale one. Honestly, I did not realize that my breathing was as shallow as labored as it was. I couldn't get it back to normal. Paranoia began to stop by and say *hello* and my "anxiousness dial" red-lined to the max. Now I'm super worried and revved up. I begin to feel my body turn itself over and twist into one of those large, soft, big Bavarian pretzels (no salt as I need to keep the BP down). Not good I thought, like the movie line from the original Top Gun when Maverick pulls out of the dog fight, "Uh… It's not good. It doesn't look good." I can hear Tom Cruise's voice and intonation in mine as I spoke those exact words out loud, repeatedly, to myself.

13

"Uh… It's not good. It doesn't look good." The shit hit the fan and it was set on high speed, pointed right at me!

I immediately alerted my kids and called my sister and brother-in-law. At this point I knew something had to be done as soon as possible, no more messing around before I become delusional and/or lose consciousness. Perhaps a major cardiac event was coming or some stroke that would leave me incapacitated (I told you that *worry* was my middle name). I lost the love of my life just over a month ago and now, would I have to leave my children and family all by themselves? (Insert very offensive swear words here please).

Our primary care physicians were in a hospital network that, of course, was not affiliated with the hospital closest to me. The risk I faced was going to a hospital that was not 'in-network' and undergo a new path of diagnosis, start from scratch, receive treatment from a different set of physicians who may have a different method to treat Covid versus going to the hospital and doctors that are up to date with me and my health. Plus, keep this in mind, I'd have to deal with all the insurance fallout from going to an out of network provider and all the small, numerous details that always get left behind.

We called our local fire department and confirmed that they could not transport me to the hospital I wanted (needed) to go to. It's New Year's Day and the dozen or so of private ambulance transport services we called were either limited in staff, couldn't reach me due to the inclement weather or had a backlog of calls extending into the next day. It wasn't going to happen. FUDGE! Formula: Please remove the letters 'DGE' from the previous word and replace it with 'CK.' I didn't swear – you just did!

This was quickly draining me, or maybe I was becoming more aware of how I felt. I began to feel warm, lightheaded, and started to run a temperature. My speech was forced as I tried to concentrate on forming the right words to produce a sentence. It's unexplainable how fear can control you emotionally and physically. The snow and sleet kept punishing the ground and causing a scene that would've made a nice 'White Christmas' just a week before. Our streets weren't plowed, it was cold, and everything was freezing as it hit the ground. We were out of options. I was out of options.

I must give a shout out to the wonderful Emergency Services Police and Fire departments from Elgin, IL. They provided me with the best option to get the fastest help. These were also the fine folks that saved my wife's life just a few years ago. They proposed that they come out on a 9-1-1 call, treat, and evaluate me onsite and then transport me if I become critical. In reality, I had no choice as they wanted to get me care ASAP. If all went well, I could then wait for the storm to lighten and have my children take me to our affiliated in-network hospital. If not, I would still be getting treatment and no longer wasting time.

I'm not sure how you feel or felt in these situations, but a bit of an embarrassment came over me. When I was a kid, I would've LOVED to ride in an ambulance or on a fire truck. But I don't want to be the one that the ambulance or fire truck is there for! After all that I have been through with my family and with my wife, the hospitals, care facilities, treatment centers, etc., you'd think I'd be acclimated to these situations. It's completely different when it's happening to YOU. I still felt like I didn't want or warrant this attention.

The paramedics were dispatched with a fire department escort to my house. In my neighborhood this is not the normal type of excitement for sure. Texts came in from those neighbors around me asking what was going on. We're also truly fortunate to have fantastic families around us. I recall barely being able to text back with my now feeble, shaky hands.

7

Darth Paramedic

The wind and snow blew steadily in through our front door as in comes a paramedic with his bags of tricks and packages of stuff that I have no idea what they do or are for. I'm so sorry that I cannot recall all the names of the people that helped me and my family – truly dedicated individuals. He's fully bundled head to toe, with gloves, boots, and a mask plus a face shield under a fireman's cap. The paramedic comes over to me and I can only see his eyes, eyebrows, and part of the top of his nose. Yep, I was waiting for him to say, (Luke) "No, I am your Father!"

At this point, I lent myself to him and to whatever was going to happen as my strength to fight had perished. It's like when you've run too far too fast in gym class or tried to run a marathon and just want to collapse when it's over to hug the ground and wait out the agony. Your vanity (and sanity) goes right out the door. No, I have never attempted to run or train for a marathon – I only liked the older candy bars.

Immediately he put an oxygen nasal cannula on me over my head. I have never experienced this but have seen it so many times in movies and on TV. I thought those nose "candles" as I called them, extended way up in your nostrils down the back of your throat and into your lungs! Well, they don't at all. He tested my pulse-ox with a professional one and it was still low. How low? He didn't say and I didn't want to ask. Blood pressure, pulse rate, temperature, lung/heart checks etc., etc. and on.

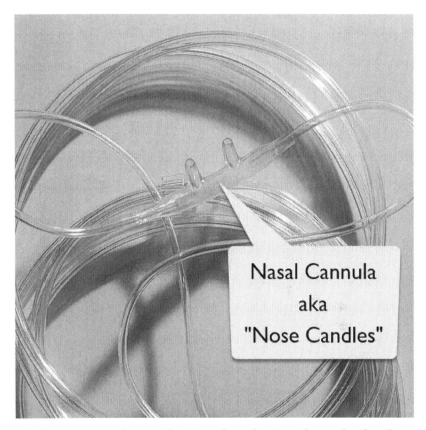

Nasal Cannula
aka
"Nose Candles"

He then instructed me to begin to breathe in and out slowly. Over the course of the next 15 to 20 minutes, my pulse-ox level began to rise. I'm not sure how much oxygen was blowing into my nose, but I appeared to breathe a bit better – I didn't feel like I was, but my numbers began to slowly elevate. This was a good sign I thought but I truly had no idea how critical I was. Much later, I was informed by several medical professionals that I was in serious, critical condition. Not getting treatment could've (would've) resulted in a major malfunction, I'll just leave it at that.

At a certain point, the paramedic offered to either transport me to the closest hospital or have my kids drive me to our hospital. The feeling that I just bought myself some time came over me. I did not feel well, no, but this was the opportunity to get to where I wanted to be for treatment. From this point, we called my physicians, and they notified the ER that we were coming in. When I first stood up, I swear that I was standing perfectly still, and the entire room was spinning around me. I thought to myself, where's the disco ball with all the flashing lights on it!

The feeling of having to rely on someone else to hold you up and support you is so unnatural for sure. I'll be darned, I felt SO weak, shaky, and drained like I hadn't stood up in weeks. Again, I kept muttering under my breath, *It's not good. It doesn't look good.* The paramedic and my son began walking me to our garage and to my car. From an outsider's perspective, this must have looked like a comedy sketch. My big-ass self being held up by my son and a paramedic navigating around the kitchen table then the narrow hallway to the garage all while having the oxygen tank and hose around me.

8

Hospital Time

O kay, so my kids drove me to the hospital late at night as the snowstorm began to lessen. Without oxygen I could feel myself declining. My son was driving and was following a path that a snowplow had just made, the other lanes were caked in slush and snow with no ruts to trace. As we were driving, I was taking in the sites and places that I never paid attention to. It's not a far drive but it takes an event like this for you to take notice of what's around you. Mentally I was aware that I had to give myself to this situation as I had done when Darth Vader the paramedic arrived. I had to find out what was wrong and then battle it. I thought at any second, I could have a seizure, blackout or pass away – just like that. You hear it all the time, life is short, life is precious, but you never take stock in it until it's you that's up to bat.

We arrive at the Emergency Room entrance and my daughter goes ahead to check me in while my son drops me off at the door and gets me a wheelchair. Me, in a wheelchair, for real? I'm used to racing with my wife's or using her Hoveround to run circles in the kitchen and chase the dog. Anyway, I got wheeled into the ER and due to restrictions at the time, my kids had to leave as I cannot be accompanied by anyone.

19

There were a few people there, but it was not crowded at all. I guess the Holiday and severe weather kept it a bit quiet for now. It didn't matter as I was immediately placed into a triage room instead of sitting with everyone else in the waiting room. Hey, carte blanche I thought. The real reason was that I was in critical condition.

I now noticed that my nose was running, I was chilled all over, and I was coughing. A rough lung and chest full of gunk cough. My mouth was dry, and my head was pounding so much that it made all my body aches not feel as bad. The triage nurse came in fully gloved, masked, paper gown on, and with shields up in case we were attacked. After all the preliminary tests, pokes and prods and questions were answered I was able to sit and wait in silence for a moment. My head leaned to my left side perched up by my left arm on the wheelchair. I thought to myself, "phone, charger, cord, glasses, clothes, and shoes" – that's all I have on me in case someone needs to recover them. Then the thoughts of, "well this is what the fear of dying must be like" were creeping in. The realization that Dorothy was right, "Toto, we're not in Kansas anymore." Just what in the Fu_dge_ (use the "ck" replacement formula above to replace the "dge" letters) was going on with me here???

9

Zoo Glass

I 'm not sure how long it was until they placed me in an ER exam room. I'm sure I didn't have to wait long at all. I slid from the wheelchair into the ER bed, then I was elevated. Next, a whirlwind of activity is going on all around me. "Hi, I'm nurse so and so," "My name is blah, blah and I'm here to do this," "Can you tell me this," "I'm going to stick this in you now, it will sting and hurt." Okay, okay – I'm in tune with it and fully cooperative. It felt as if I was frozen in place while all this action was going on around me. I understood what was going on and went with it. Then an eerie calm had come over me that wouldn't last for long. I would soon be revving the engine to peak and dropping the transmission. This would shift me into high gear as not being in control or having any input as to what is happening is one of the worst feelings you can have. Up and down, peaks and valleys. It's like flying on a commercial airliner wishing that I could be in some sort of control or at the very least – see straight ahead out the cockpit window as to where we're going or what we're about to fly into!

In comes my primary ER care nurse – super nice lady except for one thing. She's wearing what looks like a motorcycle helmet (I'm not kidding here) that has the full-face shield pulled down and has a hose coming out of the rear of the helmet to an attachment on her hip that looks like some rectangular power pack complete with lights and noise maker. I'm sure it was an air scrubber of some sort but as if my eyes weren't open wide enough to what the heck was happening, I now had to deal with the feeling that I was sequestered in a sterilized room! I wondered what happens when you fart in one of those types of rooms? Does the air and smell get filtered out or will the people on the other side of the wall still smell it. Hear it, probably. Ah Never mind.

I'm sure that at some point you have been to the zoo. If not, perhaps you've seen some of the exhibits where animals are displayed behind some sort of glass enclosure. The ER exam room I was in has this nice window in the door that has shutters on it. Mine were open. The next thing I noticed had me looking around my bed and room to try and see what all the 'eyes' were looking at. A convergence of nurses, doctors, aids, cleaning crew, enema specialists, etc., began to approach the window. They appeared to all be in sync moving slowly together up to my glass window to gaze in. Of course, it was me that they were looking at and the wall of IBM monitors behind me as if I was sitting in an air traffic control tower. I found out later that they (of course) were not gawking at me, rather they couldn't understand how I was still coherent with such a low pulse-ox reading and nearly two collapsed lungs. Another check mark for the seriousness of this event.

Now began the tests, x-rays, blood draws, questions, poking, pill taking, shots and on. Lay back, sit up, drink this, turn and cough, can you fill this cup from here? They began the process of determining the right number of liters per minute to set my oxygen to. This go around, it felt and looked like my oxygen was coming from a common garden hose right to my nose! I remained in the ER for a few hours, and I fought going to sleep thinking that I may never wake up. I sat in the ER bed, closed my eyes, and concentrated on trying to breathe normally. "Is this really happening......?"

10

A Room with No View

I n the wee hours of the morning the next day, I was transferred to a room on a critical care floor. I don't believe that there were any ICU beds available at that time and I was happy to be in a step-down unit from the ICU.

No visitors at all were allowed and I only had two windows to try and see out of. I found it funny after a while that my life for this week was going to just be these four walls. I couldn't even see the door to the room or peer into the hallway. It was as if nothing existed outside of my room. I could not get up out of bed or sit on the edge of the bed as I was considered a 'fall risk' plus I didn't have the strength to. *Battle on*, I kept telling myself. Push yourself a little bit every day and keep building on that momentum, no matter how small a gain it is, at least it's a gain.

As I lay in the hospital bed in my room, hooked up to this loud, oxygen generating machine, I stared out into the darkness of the night wondering if my kids and family were ok – that's all I could think about at the time. My own personal mourning and grief was still so fresh, but I wanted to be there for my kids so bad, not stuck here. I didn't want them taking care of me. My son and daughter had made it back home safely that night in the snow and my other daughter was in the city (safely at home). She was stuck there wishing she were with us as much as we were wishing she were here too. I also wished my wife; their mother was there for them. This is a real sad and lonely moment here – my apologies to you, the reader, for the melancholy moment.

Every nurse, doctor, cleaning crew, aid, food server, therapist, blackjack dealer, etc. all had to wear protective gear when coming into my room, even if it was for a brief moment. I came well equipped as I had a blood pressure cuff attached, garden hose of oxygen constantly blowing up my nose, an IV plus a port in my wrist and wonderfully bright green non-slip gripper socks! I then was upgraded to a "professional" pulse oximeter complete with its own transmitter. The simple finger pulse-ox reader just wasn't enough, so they taped the leads of the "Super Deluxe 10.0 version" pulse-ox reader to my ear lobe, and the transmitter went into my front gown pocket. It was heavy and the wire pulled the hospital gown down and tugged on my ear all the time. I had been poked, jabbed, and stabbed so many times that the bandage tape residue would remain on my skin for weeks after I got home.

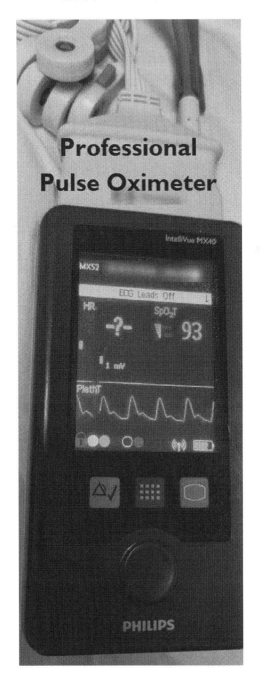

Ok, ok. Quick note here. I loved these people. They were helping me and were so kind I cannot give them enough credit for the thankless job they do. Truly I was a good patient and caused no trouble. In fact, when you're in the hospital for any length of time, you are required to have an IV port inserted in you at all times in case of any emergency. There were times when they just couldn't catch a vein and kept trying the hand, wrist, arm, etc. Strangely, I did not mind at all. You'd think you'd be at a point where you'd say "STOP!" I went for the cheerleader aspect – "C'mon you can do it. Jab it in there! You can do it!"

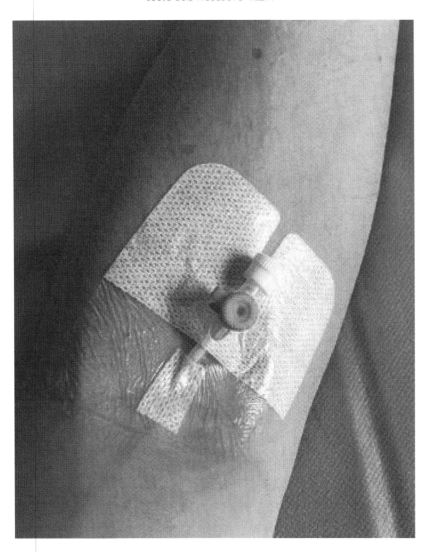

11

Prognosis Positive

The diagnosis had come in and it was official, I had Covid Pneumonia. My lungs were pure milky white on my x-rays as they were fully compromised. My pneumonia was caused by a viral (Covid) infection that filled up all the air sacs in both lung lobes with fluid and puss. I was now being handed off to numerous doctors, departments, and specialists trying to assess the damage and treatment plans. Apparently, I had been living with Covid for longer than I thought, and it developed into pneumonia. For Covid, I was well past the point for the then major approved treatments. Alternative treatments were now being considered. Holy Crap, I kept thinking. I am nearing rock bottom here. I am at rock bottom. I found myself so fatigued that at this point, I would welcome just being able to pass out for a few hours at a time to get some rest. Hourly routine well checks would disrupt any hope of a sleep cycle.

The biggest fear of all was right in front of me. The media bombardment surrounding Covid and all the research I have done brought about the question of "If I get any worse, will they consider putting me on a ventilator?" No. No. I said to myself. Then I began to say it out loud to the staff around me. The Vegas odds of staying alive after being placed on a vent were Death 100, Life Zero. Thankfully and gratefully, it did not come to that.

I was also up for a new alternative drug that was used for treating arthritis with varying side effects that could last longer than a year. There are too many named drugs that they could have used and ones that were approved for use. Some had been used in case studies each with no long-term data to back it up. I know you have heard of most of them. But, for me, (of course), I was way too far along in the Covid process that it was determined the best course for action was to treat the pneumonia and all my other symptoms and ride the virus out. A strong and facetious "Just effing great" popped out of my mouth.

12

Baseball, Arnold, and Cows

S teroid injections have historically been used for many odd purposes. Steroids are one of the best ways to treat pneumonia. These injections elevate your blood sugar levels. I'm not a full-blown diabetic, but the injection battle began. Injections in the stomach that is. It starts with a steroid injection followed by a blood test followed by an insulin injection. The vicious circle to find the correct balance of steroid to insulin ratio became a daily fight. I thought, at first, they would be injecting me in my "behind" similar to how the sports athletes allegedly were. I worried that I would begin to build muscle and my testicles would shrink and then I'd start to moo!

Next – I was told that I had to lay on my stomach as much as possible. This was the best thing for my lungs to heal. I can barely turn feeling the way I was and with everything that was attached to me, but somehow, I forced myself to turn over. From what I was told, the best position to drain your lungs is on your belly as the lungs attach to the inside of your back allowing them to expand fully down and open. Believe it or not, one of the better ways to induce air into your lungs is also singing. Yes, karaoke pneumonia was going to help me. This came from a highly qualified infectious disease doctor, and I tried my best to keep talking and singing. Oh, the horror of anyone within an earshot of my room.

I told you I am a big guy but now my weight was beginning to drop rapidly. This is an add-on bonus thing to worry about in case you don't have enough going on. Actually, this rapid weight loss would affect me over the next few months as I became a bit delusional and lightheaded. My blood pressure has always been elevated at every doctor office I've ever been to since I was 10. The White Coats are coming! "White-coat" hypertension I'm told is what this is. Even entering a hospital or medical facility would give me this uneasy feeling and I'd begin to tighten up. Well, this whole experience wiped that right out of me as I've never had such good/normal BP readings in my life every time I go for a doctor visit.

I found it very difficult to eat, so everyday I'd order a banana with my small meal. It was easier to consume and good for me I thought. After a day or two, of course – you guessed it; my blood tests were now showing high potassium levels! Oh, my goodness I am driving in a car on a multi lane highway and have managed to find every pothole going both directions.

13

Bathroom Ballet

Bathroom breaks were not on my mind. However, I was given the wonderful male urinal 'chug-jug' (as I call it), to use. When you can't move or twist with all the hoses, wires and foreign gadgets attached, this is not easy to deal with or use. I know if I laugh while attempting to dock the space station to the capsule it's going to be, "Houston, we're losing a lot of fluid here." Plus, after you are done you have to secure the cap on top and begin to work things back into place and cover back up - all with shaking hands. This is not fun, but I was grateful that I was not required to be catheterized. I'm not even going to touch that.

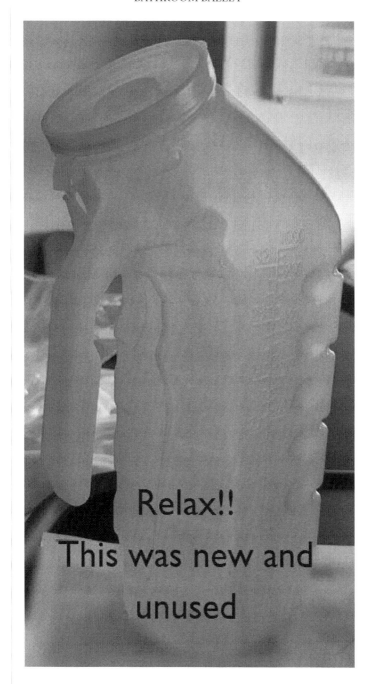

Eventually, better movement came back to me, sitting in a chair and standing up, then attempting to use the bathroom with assistance at first. It was tough trying to stand and then work my way into the bathroom.

The bathroom, which was only a few steps away, felt like it was at the top of Kilimanjaro. I said to myself, "let the dance begin." I had to sit on the edge of the bed, hold the IV pole that had the oxygen machine on it, plant my green-colored-gripper-socked feet on the ground and start to push off as if I was a skier at the top gate ready to tackle a great slalom course. Next, I'd align the power cord so it didn't get tangled in the wheels or around the pole, adjust the oxygen cord to my nose "candles" and then try to keep the gown from slipping down from the weight of the pulse-oximeter which began to tug on the wire pulling my earlobe. Plus, the great "outback" was wide open! I tried to use the pole for leverage and have the other hand free to hold on to the wall or bathroom door but, naturally it's me, I realized that the 5 wheels on the IV pole were very fluid and had no breaks on them. I slowly started to feel the wheels of the pole taking me in one direction while my body was trending the opposite way. The more force I put on the IV pole the more it wanted to go in the wrong direction. The gripper socks were now working against me as I couldn't slide my feet to adjust back around. "Splits-ville" here I come to visit you! Thankfully, the area was small and the IV pole wheels stuck against the wall and I was able to limp into the bathroom.

I hear all of you out there screaming, "Call the nurse", or "Hit the call button." There was no call button within reach as I had trapped myself in the position I was in. I do thank you for the consideration.

14

Home sweet home

As the week progressed, my body began trending in the right direction. Less attachments, hoses, less beeping and noise and less being checked on every so often. At the very end of the week, I started physical gait therapy in my room which consisted of walking from the window to the door and back again. Baby steps for sure. As my pulse-ox readings became consistently over a 90% threshold, I was nearing the end of my stay but was nowhere near being healed.

Finally I was ready to be discharged. I got myself dressed as best as I could. Phone, check, glasses, check. I rolled up the phone charger and its cord, placed them in a bag then donned the lovely green, gripper hospital socks and put on my shoes. No one would need to come and collect them. I now awaited my wheelchair chariot to take me home along with my new big green bottle of oxygen.

I arrived home and needed help getting out of the car and up the three stairs from the garage floor into the house. I found my place on the couch and dropped. I was completely and utterly defeated physically, mentally, and emotionally. I have never felt so tired in my entire life. Pure exhaustion.

I came home with several sheets of directions that I had to follow, various test kits, and more medicines than I knew what to do with. A Home oxygen concentrator was delivered, and I slowly started my road to recovery. I had to keep a chart of the medicines I took and all my test readings and then adjust accordingly.

From this point, it will take me some three months to regain some semblance of strength. It took several weeks for me to try and get up the stairs to my own bedroom. Six full months have passed since my hospital stay and I am feeling much better. I flirt with saying that I am 100% overall. My lungs have healed to the point where no evidence can be found I even had pneumonia. Truly a remarkable sign!

15

Conclusion

Fiirst off, I want to thank YOU, the reader, for sticking with me all this way. Also, a big shout of thanks goes to all the medical staff and professionals I've encountered that have helped me "run" against Covid.

Do you know some folks that have not even batted an eye with the spread of Covid? How about some that have gone to the extreme and wear masks while driving in their car, windows up with no one else with them? While I've tried to encompass all these views – we must realize that we cannot judge nor dictate to anyone, and that's tough. The difficulty also exists in those that try to impose their own wisdom and beliefs on you. This can also lead (unknowingly at times) to placing stress upon us or those around us – another factor in fighting any disease.

I hope I have enlightened you a bit and made you smile or even laugh. I appreciate you and thank you for helping me yell, "RUN COVID, RUN AWAY!"

As always, if you found this book to be helpful or entertaining, I would be very appreciative if you left a favorable review for the book on Amazon!!

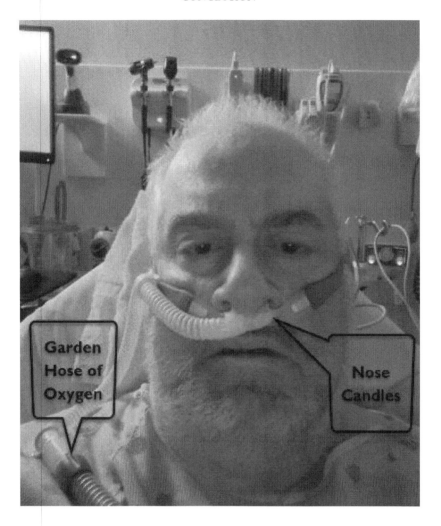

16

Resources

Z acurate Pro Series Fingertip Pulse Oximeter. (n.d.). Zacurate Pulse Oximeter. Retrieved July 6, 2022, from https://zacura te.com/products/500dl-fingertip-pulse-oximeter-black

Scott, T. (Director). (1986). *Top Gun* [Film]. Paramount Pictures

Lucas, G. (Director). (1977). *Star Wars* [Film]. Lucasfilm Ltd.

Fleming, V. (Director). (1939). *The Wizard of Oz* [Film]. Metro-Goldwyn-Mayer

Philips IntelliVue MX40. (n.d.). Philips Healthcare. Retrieved July 7, 2022, from https://www.usa.philips.com/healthcare/product/HC865350/ intellivue-mx40-patient-wearable-monitor#documents

Mayo Staff Clinicians. (2020, June 13). Pneumonia - Symptoms and causes. Mayo Clinic. Retrieved July 8, 2022, from https://www.mayoclinic.org/ diseases-conditions/pneumonia/symptoms-causes/syc-20354204

Made in the USA
Monee, IL
25 September 2022

14626614R00026